You Can Draw

ANIMALS

James Mravec

pil

Publications International, Ltd.

CONTENTS

Louis Weber, CEO
Publications International, Ltd.
7373 North Cicero Avenue
Lincolnwood, Illinois 60712

Permission is never granted for commercial purposes.

ISBN-13: 978-1-4127-1076-3
ISBN-10: 1-4127-1076-6

Manufactured in China.

8 7 6 5 4 3 2 1

How to Draw Animals

Drawing can be fun! It's not as hard as you might expect. One of the secrets of drawing is that any object can be broken down into its smaller parts. Follow the step-by-step instructions in this book, and you'll soon be drawing animals of all sorts.

You'll need some basic tools before you begin. Be sure you have a pencil, a pencil sharpener, an eraser, a felt-tip pen, and, of course, the grid paper where you'll make your drawings. Before you begin, make copies of the grid paper located on the inside of the covers of this book.

Each drawing is shown on a grid. The grid is a tool to make copying the drawings easier. Look closely at how the lines and shapes fit on the grid—watch where the lines come close to the grids and where they cross over them. Try to copy the lines exactly on your grid.

The instructions in these pages always start with larger basic shapes, such as ovals, rectangles, and triangles. Draw the full shape, even if some of it will not be seen in the final drawing. (Later, you'll erase the parts you don't need.) Each step adds more detail. The red lines in each illustration show exactly what to draw in that step, while the lines drawn in previous steps are shown in gray.

After all the steps are drawn, use a felt-tip pen to go over the pencil lines. Ink only the lines you want to keep in the final drawing. After giving the felt-tip ink some time to dry so it won't smear, use an eraser to erase the extra pencil lines.

You've finished your drawing! Now you're ready to move on to the next step: adding color.

Adding Color

Now that the line art is finished, it's time to color the drawing. You can use any coloring tools you like: If you enjoy coloring with crayons, use them. Later you can try other mediums, such as colored pencils, watercolors, markers, or colored chalk. Try different techniques on the drawings to see what looks best.

Pick colors that fit the subject of the drawing. Start by adding the main color to the drawing. Keep the colors light at first. After you are finished with the main color, gently add darker colors to areas that would be in shadows or less light (generally toward the bottom or underneath the shapes). This is called *shading*. After shading the drawing, add lighter colors where more light would be (usually on the top areas of the shapes, where sunlight would naturally hit them). This is called *highlighting*. Shading and highlighting help the drawing to look more dimensional, or realistic. Look at the pictures in the book, and try to copy the shading and highlighting of each color.

Once you fill in all the colors and are pleased with the way it looks, your illustration is complete. Way to go!

DOG

1. Draw a kidney-bean shape for the body. Add ovals for the head and snout.

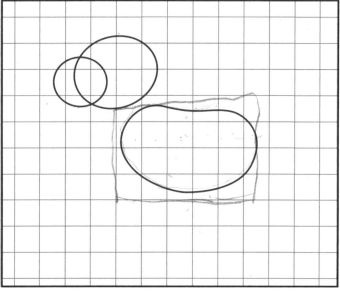

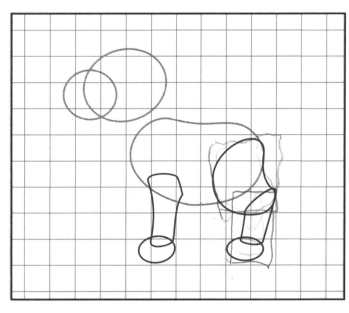

2. On the dog's near side, draw the shapes for one front leg and one back leg, and add ovals for the paws.

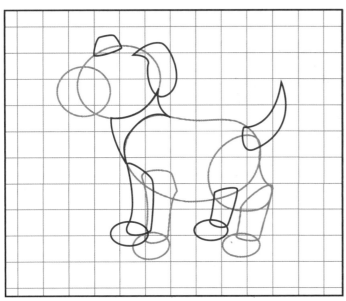

3. Draw curved shapes for the ears. Connect the head to the body with curved lines, and add more curved lines for the tail. Draw the shapes for the two legs on the other side, and add ovals for the paws.

4. Draw ovals for the eyes, pupils, and nose. Add spots on the dog's body, tail, and ear. Put in more curved lines for details of the mouth, the toes, and the hair on the dog's head.

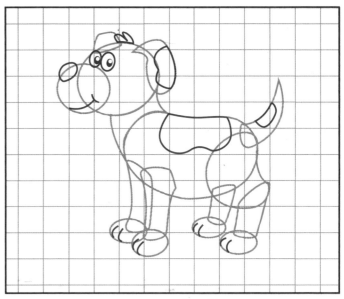

5. Trace the pencil lines you want to keep with a felt-tip pen, and erase any extra lines.

Cat

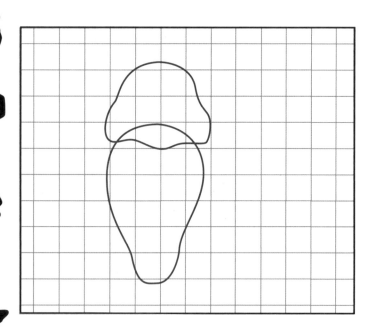

1. Draw an upside-down pear shape for the body, and add the head shape.

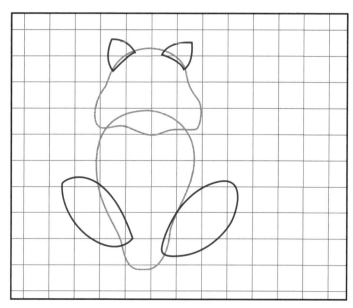

2. Sketch two football shapes for the legs. Add two rounded triangles for the ears.

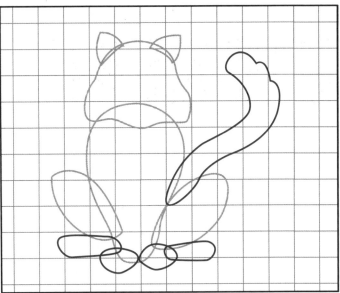

3. Draw a curved shape for the tail. Put in short ovals for the front paws and curved rectangles for the back paws.

4. Draw ovals for the eyes, and add smaller ones for the pupils. Sketch a triangle for the nose with curved lines underneath it for the mouth. Put smaller triangles inside the ear shapes. Add curved lines for eyebrows and eyelashes and details on the toes, hair, legs, tail, and whiskers.

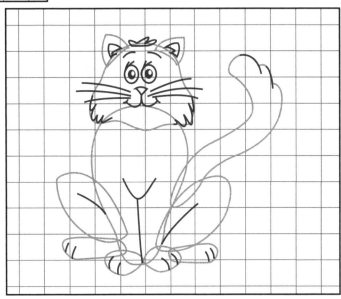

5. Trace the pencil lines you want to keep with a felt-tip pen, and erase any extra lines.

GOLDFISH

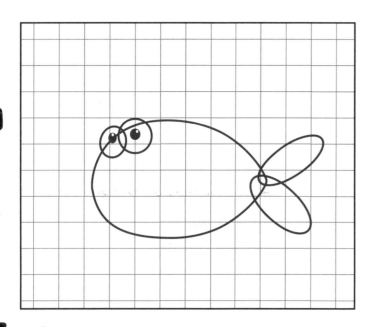

1. Start with a sideways teardrop for the body. Draw two ovals at one end for the tail. Add more ovals or circles for the eyes and pupils.

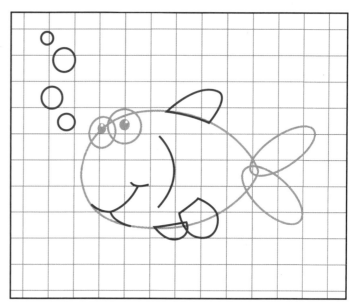

2. Draw three fin shapes, one on top and two on the bottom. Add some circles for bubbles, and draw curves for the gills and mouth.

To complete each animal, go through the steps in order.

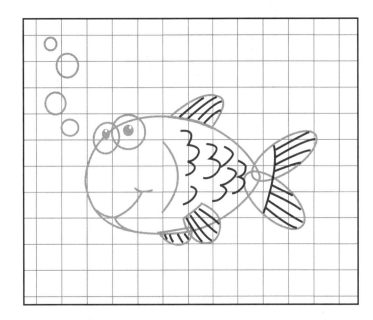

3. Add curved lines for the scales on the side. Draw lines for the details on the fins.

4. Use a felt-tip pen to trace over the lines you want to keep, and erase the extra pencil lines.

FROG

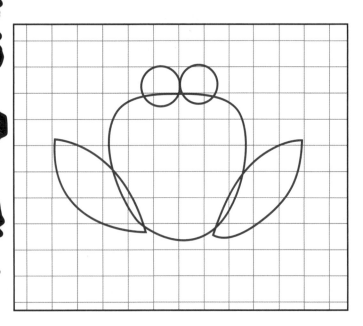

1. Draw an apple shape for the body, and add two circles at the top for the eyes. Put in two football shapes for the legs.

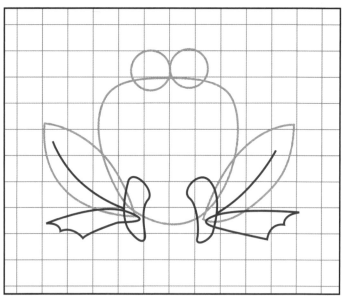

2. Draw the arm shapes and the webbed back feet. Add curved lines for the leg details.

3. Draw small circles for the eye pupils. Add hand shapes, and draw circles for details on the skin. Put in curved lines for the mouth, back feet, and eyebrows.

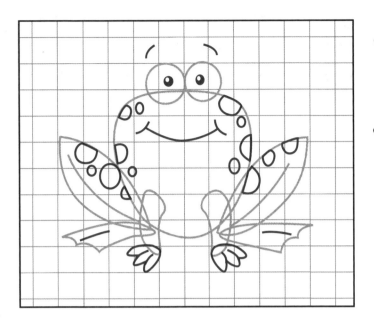

4. Use a felt-tip pen to trace over the lines you want to keep, and erase the extra pencil lines.

Use a clean eraser to remove pencil lines. This helps avoid pencil smudges on the paper.

HORSE

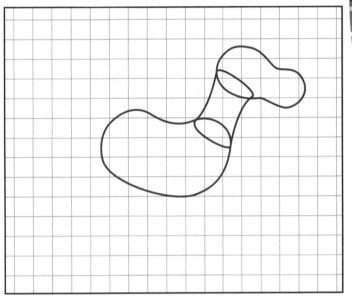

1. Draw a kidney-bean shape for the body and a peanut shape for the head. Add a rectangular form between them for the neck.

2. Draw the two front legs. Sketch the closest back leg in two pieces, one pear shape and one rectangular shape. Add a rectangular shape for the back leg on the far side of the horse. Put in ovals for the ears.

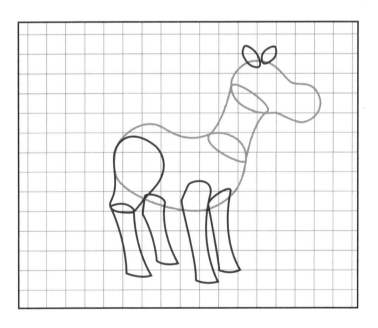

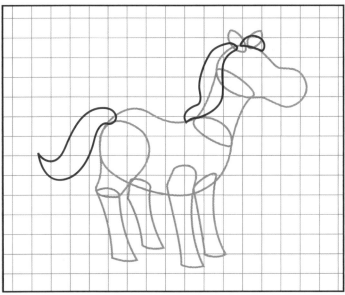

3. Draw two long S shapes for the tail and mane. Add the small mane on top of the head.

4. Draw ovals for the eyes, nostrils, and ear details. Put pupils in the eyes. Add hooves at the bottom of each leg. Finish this step with lines for the mouth, tail, and mane details.

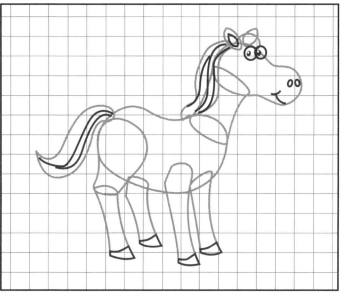

5. Use a felt-tip pen to trace over the lines you want to keep, and erase the extra pencil lines.

COW

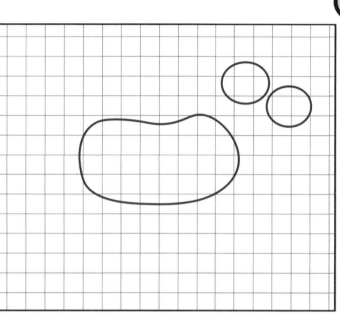

1. Draw two slightly flat circles for the head and nose. Add a kidney-bean shape for the body.

2. Draw a rounded rectangle for the neck, connecting the head, nose, and body. Add a long shape for the front leg on the near side. Draw the shape for the top of the back leg on the near side, connecting it to the body. Add a rectangle for the lower leg.

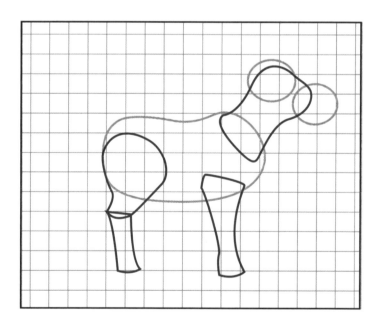

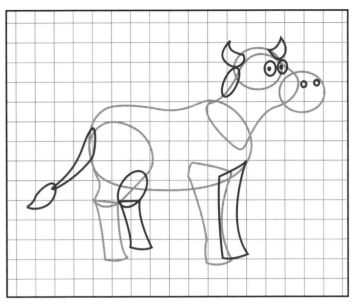

3. Draw a long shape for the front leg on the far side. Draw a small oval for the top of the back leg on the far side, and add a rectangle for the lower leg. Put in a curved shape for the tail, and sketch a teardrop shape at the end of it. Add ovals for the eyes, nostrils, and ear. Add pupils inside the eyes. Draw two horn shapes.

4. Draw hooves at the bottom of each leg. Put in curved lines for mouth, tail, and hoof details. Add spots in any pattern you like.

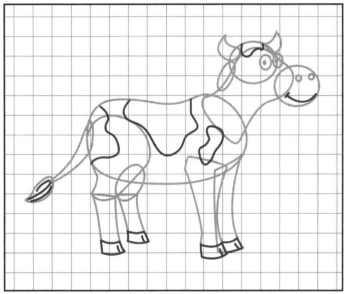

5. Trace the lines you want to keep with a felt-tip pen, and erase the extra lines.

PIG

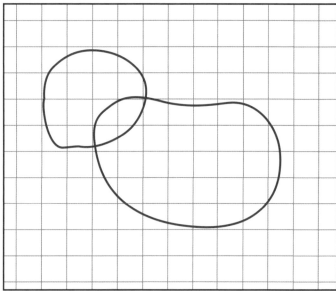

1. Draw a kidney-bean shape for the body. Add an oval for the head, but put a lump on it for the chin.

2. Draw two short, rounded rectangles for the legs. Add another for the snout, and sketch a squiggly shape for the tail.

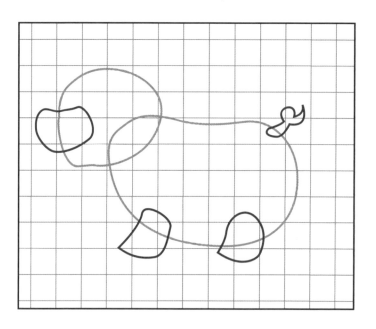

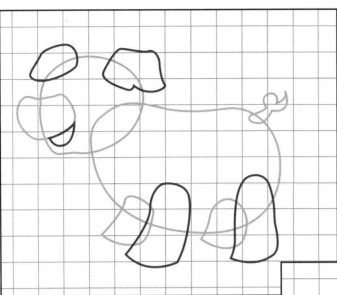

3. Draw the other two legs on the near side, and add shapes for the ears and mouth.

4. Draw hoof shapes at the end of the legs, and add triangles for detail. Sketch in the end of the snout, and add ovals for the eyes and nostrils. Finish with curved lines for eyebrows, hair, cheek, ear, and tail detail.

5. Trace the pencil lines you want to keep with a felt-tip pen, and erase any extra lines.

PENGUIN

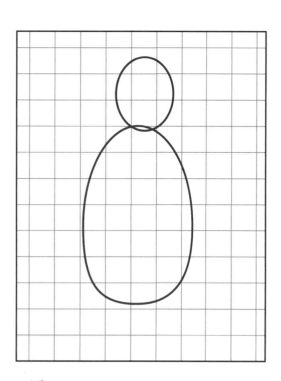

1. Draw a long egg shape for the body and then an oval for the head.

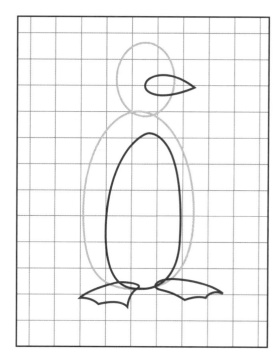

2. Draw a thinner egg shape inside the first one for the belly. Add a teardrop beak and two webbed feet.

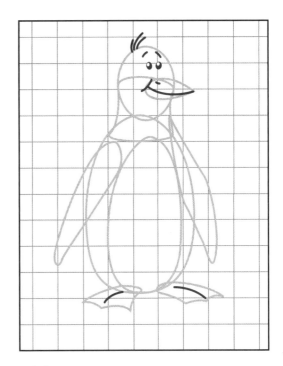

3. Draw the flippers and the neck shape.

4. Draw ovals for the eyes. Add a line to each webbed foot for detail. Finish this step with curved lines for the mouth, nostril, eyebrows, and feathers on top of the head.

Remember that the red lines show the new steps you need to draw.

5. Use a felt-tip pen to trace the lines you want to keep, and erase the extra pencil lines.

DOLPHIN

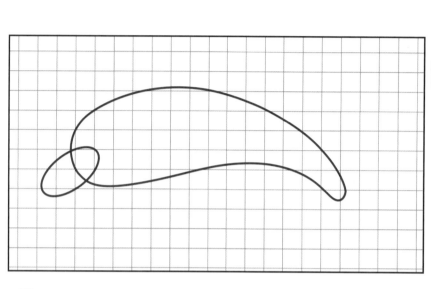

1. Draw a curved teardrop for the body and an oval for the snout.

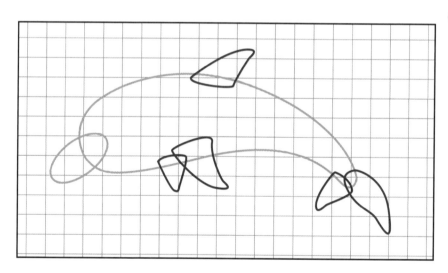

2. Add five triangular shapes for the fins: one on top, one on each side, and two at the end for the tail.

3. Draw circles for the eye and an oval at the top of the head for the blowhole. Add curved lines for the mouth.

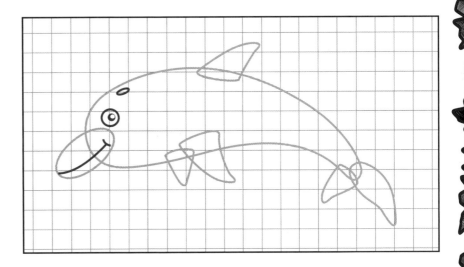

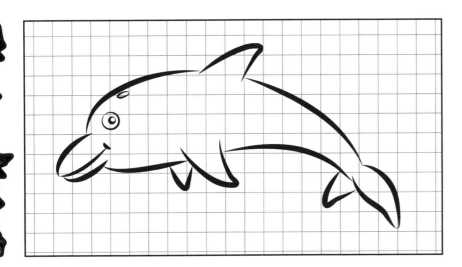

4. Use a felt-tip pen to trace the lines you want to keep, and erase the extra pencil lines.

Draw lightly with the pencil. It will be easier to erase after you've finished the felt-tip pen lines.

ALLIGATOR

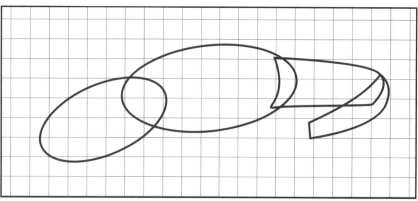

1. Draw a large oval for the body, then a smaller oval for the head and snout. Add two rounded rectangular shapes for the curving tail.

2. Add more ovals for the top of the head, the nose, and the upper part of each leg on this side.

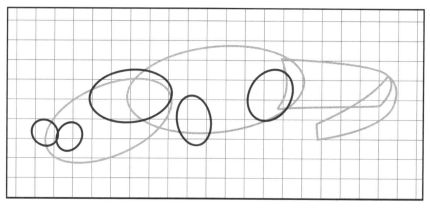

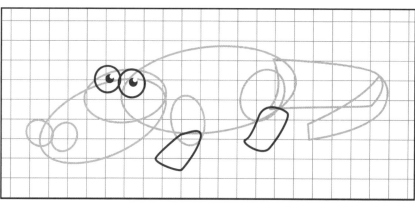

3. Draw rounded rectangles for the lower legs. Sketch two circles with black dots in the center for the eyes. Don't forget to include the white dot in the pupils.

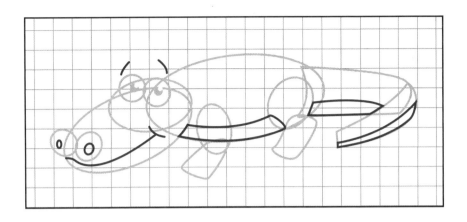

4. Add ovals for the nostrils. Draw curved lines for the mouth, eyebrows, and underside of belly, and tail.

5. Sketch triangle shapes for the claws. Add lines on the belly and tail to show scales. Draw a bumpy line along the back and top of the tail for more scale details.

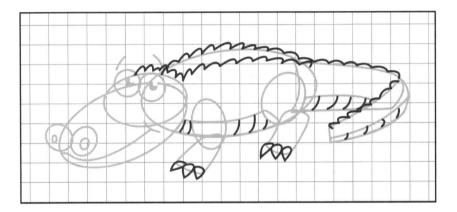

6. Use a felt-tip pen to trace over the lines you want to keep, and erase the extra pencil lines.

MONKEY

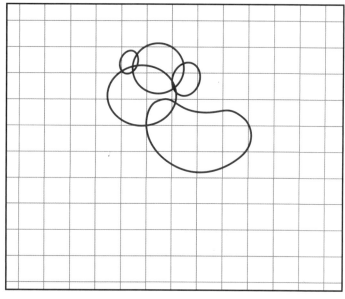

1. Draw a kidney-bean shape for the body. Add an overlapping oval and circle for the face and the head. Draw two more ovals, one on either side of the head, for ears.

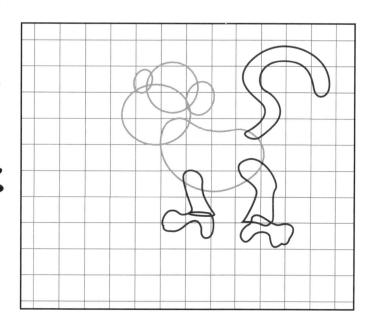

2. Draw a curving, snakelike shape for the tail. Add two long shapes from the bottom of the body for legs. Sketch the feet (don't forget that monkeys' feet look like hands).

3. Add two more curved shapes for the arms. At the end of the arms, draw the shapes for the hands.

4. Draw ovals for the eyes, pupils, and nostrils. Add a crescent shape for the mouth. Sketch curved lines for eyebrow, nose, and hair details. Put details in the ears, mouth, fingers, and toes.

5. Trace the pencil lines you want to keep with a felt-tip pen, and erase any extra lines.

ELEPHANT

1. Draw an oval for the body and an overlapping circle for the head.

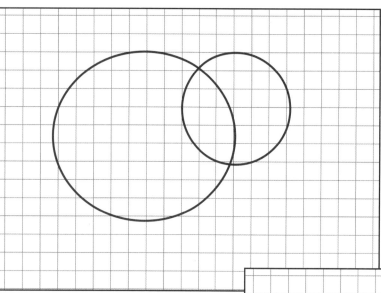

2. Draw four slightly curved rectangular shapes for the legs. Then add two triangles with rounded corners for the ears.

3. Sketch some curved lines for the tail and trunk. Put an oval shape at the end of the tail, and add two boomerang shapes next to the trunk for the tusks, one on each side.

4. Draw ovals for the eyes and the pupils. Add some curved shapes below the trunk and tusks to show the jaw and mouth. Add details on the ears, toes, and trunk. Draw eyelashes and some hair on the head.

5. Use a felt-tip pen to trace over the lines you want to keep in the drawing, and erase the extra pencil lines.

27

LION

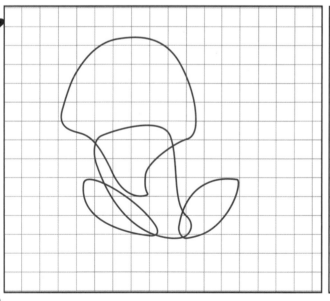

1. Draw an upside-down teardrop shape for the body. The top of the body should be flat. Add two long football shapes for the legs. Draw the head shape.

2. Draw two shapes for the lower legs and paws. Add two ears and a shape for the face.

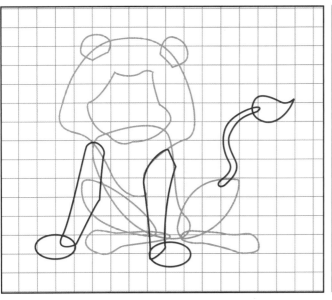

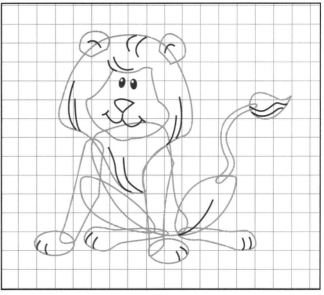

3. Draw long, rectangular shapes for the front legs. Add ovals at the bottom for the paws. Draw matching long S-curve lines, rounded together at the top and bottom, for the tail. Add a teardrop shape at its end.

4. Draw two small ovals for the eyes and a rounded triangle for the nose. Add detail lines for the ears, mouth, leg, and toes. Finish this step with lines for hair details in the mane and tail.

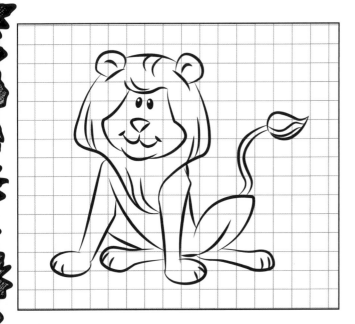

5. Trace the lines you want to keep with a felt-tip pen, and erase the extra lines.

TIGER

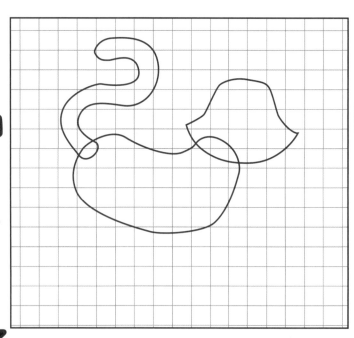

1. Draw a kidney-bean shape for the body and a squat bell shape for the head. Add a backward S shape for the tail.

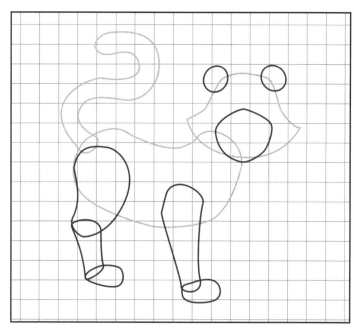

2. Draw the leg forms on the near side of the body, and add ovals for the ears and paws. Sketch a circle shape for the snout.

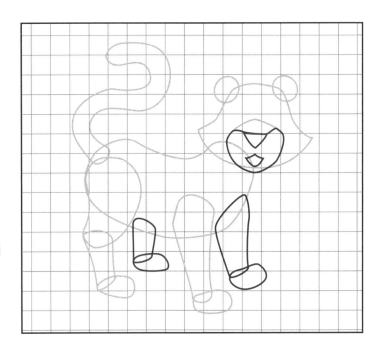

3. Draw the shapes for the legs on the other side of the body, and add ovals for the paws. Put in a snout, and add a triangle nose and a mouth shape.

Add shadows under animals and objects. This helps make them appear to stand on the ground.

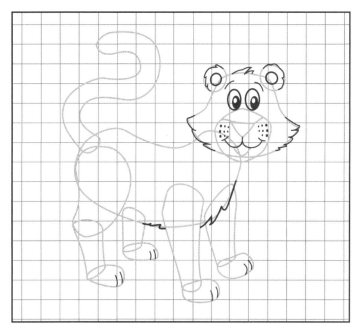

4. Draw ovals for the eyes and circles for the inner ears. Add details to the eyes and curved lines for the eyebrows, mouth, and toes. Put in spots next to the nose for whiskers. Add hair lines on the head, ears, chest, stomach, and cheeks.

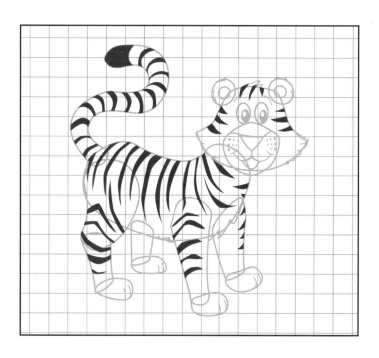

5. Draw stripes over the body, legs, tail, and head.

6. Use a felt-tip pen to trace the lines you want to keep, and erase the extra pencil lines.

Light colors can be used for making highlights when you color. This helps make the art look three-dimensional.